# contents

Introduction .......
Using the Worksheets
Setting Up Learning Centers .................
Worksheets

- ***A*** ............................................... 11
- ***B*** ............................................... 14
- ***C*** ............................................... 17
- ***D*** ............................................... 21
- ***E*** ............................................... 25
- ***F*** ............................................... 28
- ***G*** ............................................... 32
- ***H*** ............................................... 35
- ***I*** ............................................... 38
- ***J*** ............................................... 42
- ***K*** ............................................... 45
- ***L*** ............................................... 48
- ***M*** ............................................... 51
- ***N*** ............................................... 54
- ***O*** ............................................... 57
- ***P*** ............................................... 60
- ***Q*** ............................................... 63
- ***R*** ............................................... 66
- ***S*** ............................................... 70
- ***T*** ............................................... 73
- ***U*** ............................................... 76
- ***V*** ............................................... 79
- ***W*** ............................................... 82
- ***X*** ............................................... 86
- ***Y*** ............................................... 90
- ***Z*** ............................................... 93

# introduction

*Letters A–Z* is designed to enhance primary education through the use of manipulatives and tactile materials. The learning activities help students develop visual, auditory, kinesthetic, tactile, and perceptual skills while providing opportunities for creative expression. Although students may appear to be participating in art projects, they are, in fact, achieving artistically such curriculum objectives as recognizing uppercase and lowercase letters, writing letters, associating letters with beginning sounds, and developing eye-hand coordination and fine motor skills.

The worksheets contained here are structured to allow repetition when learning new concepts—an approach that educators have noted is essential for internalizing concepts and skills. The learning materials are specifically designed to appeal to young children and to provide them with the positive reinforcement they need for learning new skills.

Worksheet-based activities require minimal teacher preparation and can be used with students working individually, in small groups, or in independent learning centers. Most of these activities use common school supplies such as crayons, scissors, and glue or paste. Some activities require additional materials that are inexpensive and readily available in many classrooms or from art supply stores.

To administer an activity, assemble and distribute the necessary materials. (Materials lists, along with suggestions for variations, extensions, and enrichment activities, are provided in the section called "Using the Worksheets.") Read the worksheet instructions aloud to the students and make sure they understand what to do. Provide help as needed (especially with stapling art), and always supervise the use of scissors and glue.

We hope you enjoy using this book and, most of all, that it makes learning fun for your students.

# Apples 🍎🍎 for Teachers
A Basic Skills Reinforcement Program for Young Children

by
Diane Burkle
Cynthia Polk Muller
and
Linda J. Petuch

**Fearon Teacher Aids**
Belmont, California

Illustrator: Pauline Phung
Cover illustration by: Marilynn G. Barr

Entire contents copyright © 1988 by Fearon Teacher Aids,
500 Harbor Boulevard, Belmont, California 94002. However,
the individual purchaser may reproduce designated materials
in this book for classroom and individual use, but the purchase
of this book does not entitle reproduction of any part for an
entire school, district, or system. Such use is strictly prohibited.

ISBN 0-8224-0456-7

Printed in the United States of America

1. 9 8 7 6 5

# using the worksheets

There are three worksheets to teach each letter, A through Z. After your students have completed one or two worksheets of a kind, they may be able to complete the others of that kind without instructions. Use the following notes to help you administer each kind of worksheet:

## learning letters
(pp. 11, 14, 17, 21, 25, 28, 32, 35, 38, 42, 45, 48, 51, 54, 57, 60, 63, 66, 70, 73, 76, 79, 82, 86, 90, and 93)

**objectives and skills**
Recognizing letter shapes
Developing left-to-right orientation
Developing fine motor skills

**materials**  crayons

**variations**

✓ You may wish to have the children do a crayon-resist activity (painting over the crayoned letters) instead of just coloring the letters. If so, encourage them to use dark crayons, to press hard while coloring, and to fill in all areas of the letter outlines.

✓ Instead of having students color the letter outlines, have them fill the inside of the letters with glue or paste and sprinkle sand, glitter, dry macaroni or dried peas or beans, torn pieces of colorful paper, or any other materials over the wet glue. It is a good idea to have the children use glue sticks instead of glue or paste. Glue sticks are available at most stationery stores or art supply stores, they are convenient, and they keep artwork (and children's hands!) neat and clean. When children use glue sticks to fill in the letter outlines, they may actually be simulating letter-writing.

**extensions**  ✓ Have students cut out the letters and paste them on a contrasting background, such as colored construction paper.

✓ Have students cut out their letters and use them as patterns for tracing.

✓ Create a bulletin board display of cutout letters, allowing students to sort the letters by uppercase and lowercase letters and to arrange them in order as they are learned.

**enrichment**  ✓ Introduce the sound of each letter with examples of words that begin with the letter or contain the letter.

✓ Initiate a guessing game in which students determine if a word you name contains a given letter.

✓ Encourage students to name words on their own that begin with a given letter.

✓ Have the children act out each letter as they learn it, forming letter shapes with their bodies.

# writing letters
(pp. 12, 15, 18, 22, 26, 29, 33, 36, 39, 43, 46, 49, 52, 55, 58, 61, 64, 67, 71, 74, 77, 80, 83, 87, 91, and 94)

**objectives and skills**  Identifying letter shapes
Recognizing likenesses and differences
Associating initial sounds with letters
Developing eye-hand coordination
Developing fine motor skills

**materials**  crayons or colored pencils
glue
glitter

**extensions**  ✓ Have the students find given letters in old newspapers or magazines, either circling the letters or cutting them out and gluing them to their papers.

✓ Provide writing paper for additional practice in printing letters.

✓ Capable students may be able to copy the sentence that appears on the worksheet.

✓ Provide students with letter stencils and paper to reinforce letter shapes.

✓ Have students cut out the illustration on the worksheet and, in cooperative groups, create montages.

**enrichment**  ✓ Ask students to name an animal or an object that begins with the given letter, then draw a picture of it and print the letter.

# fun with letters
(pp. 13, 16, 19-20, 23-24, 27, 30-31, 34, 37, 40-41, 44, 47, 50, 53, 56, 59, 62, 65, 68-69, 72, 75, 78, 81, 84-85, 88-89, 92, and 95-96)

**objectives and skills**  Reinforcing letter-sound recognition
Developing creativity
Developing fine motor skills
Developing direction-following skills, using pictorial and auditory directions

**variation**  ✓ Most worksheet pictures can be decorated using a variety of materials in addition to those suggested below. Optional materials may include dry macaroni, birdseed, confetti, paper "holes" from a hole punch, fabric scraps, torn or cut construction paper, wallpaper scraps, sequins, buttons, felt, colored tape, and adhesive stickers such as stars and dots.

**extension**  ✓ Display the finished artwork on a bulletin board or on a table or shelf in your classroom.

**enrichment**  ✓ Ask students to describe their artwork using words that contain the given letter.

**materials (per student)**

**A** is for alligator *(p. 13)*
crayons
scissors

**B** is for beach ball *(p. 16)*
crayons
colored tissue paper cut into 2-inch squares
glue

**C** is for cow *(pp. 19–20)*
crayons
scissors
paper lunch bag
glue

**D** is for doll *(pp. 23–24)*
crayons
scissors
stapler
20–25 small cotton balls

**E** is for elephant *(p. 27)*
crayons
scissors

**F** is for flower *(pp. 30–31)*
crayons
scissors
glue or paste

**G** is for goldfish *(p. 34)*
crayons
orange tissue paper cut into 2-inch squares
glue or paste

**H** is for house *(p. 37)*
crayons
scissors
glue or paste

**I** is for inchworm *(pp. 40–41)*
crayons
scissors
glue or paste

**J** is for jellyfish *(p. 44)*
crayons
seven 4-inch lengths of yarn
glue or paste

**K** is for kite *(p. 47)*
crayons
scissors
one 6-inch length of yarn
two or three fabric scraps in strips
glue or paste

**L** is for lobster *(p. 50)*
crayons
glue
glitter

**M** is for mouse *(p. 53)*
crayons
scissors
glue or paste
one 5-inch and three ½-inch lengths of yarn

**N** is for necklace *(p. 56)*
crayons
colored tissue paper cut into 2-inch squares
glue

**O** is for ostrich *(p. 59)*
crayons
scissors
12-inch by 18-inch construction or butcher paper
two 5-inch and one 3-inch lengths of yarn
several feathers

**P** is for pig *(p. 62)*
crayons
scissors
8½-inch by 11-inch construction or butcher paper
glue

**Q** is for queen *(p. 65)*
crayons
sequins
glitter

**R** is for rabbit *(pp. 68–69)*
crayons
scissors
paper lunch bag
glue or paste
six 3-inch lengths of yarn
cotton ball

**S** is for snake *(p. 72)*
crayons
scissors

**T** is for turtle *(p. 75)*
crayons
scissors

**U** is for underwater *(p. 78)*
crayons
water colors
shallow containers
paintbrush

**materials (per student)**
continued

**V is for volcano** *(p. 81)*
crayons
glue
colored tissue paper cut into
  2-inch squares
pencil
sand

**W is for witch** *(pp. 84–85)*
crayons
scissors
12-inch by 18-inch construction or butcher paper
glue
eight 2-inch lengths of yarn

**X is for xylophone** *(pp. 88–89)*
crayons
scissors
glue or paste

**Y is for yak** *(p. 92)*
yellow crayons
ten to fifteen ½-inch to 2-inch
  lengths of yellow yarn

**Z is for zebra** *(pp. 95–96)*
crayons
scissors
paper lunch bag
glue or paste

# setting up learning centers

The worksheet-based activities in this book may be adapted to a learning center environment. Nearly every worksheet focuses on a separate letter, and the worksheets are usually repeated (sometimes with slight variation) for every letter. Hence, even young children who cannot yet read may be able to work at a learning center, without teacher direction, completing worksheets on their own or in small groups. Here are some suggestions that may help you in setting up learning centers in your classroom:

**1** Set up a separate learning center for each subject area. Identify the center by hanging a symbol, such as a letter, over the table set up for that learning center.

**2** Gather materials that students will need for the activity. Place those materials in boxes or other appropriate containers, and label the containers with the word and a picture of the item contained. Store these containers in the learning center.

**3** For activities requiring paint, glue, or paste, tape a protective covering over the learning center table. Keep the covering on the table as long as that learning center continues to be used.

**4** Prepare samples of the activities. Post the samples on the bulletin board or in the learning center so that students can refer to them.

**5** Explain each different activity before the students begin working on their own. You may need to review the directions on a daily basis.

**6** If you have a few learning centers set up, students may work at the centers in rotation. Group students by ability, by compatibility, or in some random fashion. Create a chart that shows who is in each group, and post the chart on a bulletin board. Create tags that match the learning center symbols (see suggestion 1), and pin a different tag next to each group listed on the chart. The tag will tell the group which center they should go to that day. Change the tags each day.

Some activities are especially appropriate for cooperative learning situations. You may wish to assign roles, such as gathering materials, cleaning up after the activity, collecting the worksheets and making sure group members have written their names on their papers, and so on. You might also want to provide an appropriate social goal such as working quietly, asking group members for help, and so on.

**7** Provide adequate space for the completed worksheets to dry, if they have just been glued, pasted, or painted. Try not to stack or overlap the worksheets while they dry.

Learning Aa

Name _____

Color the letters below.

Name _____

Writing Aa

Look at the sentence below.
Trace each **A** and **a** that you can find.

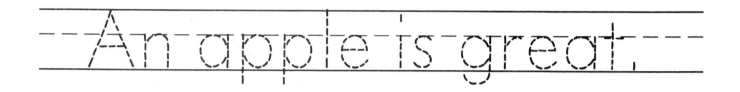

Color the apple.
Print **A** and **a** beside the apple.
Put glue on the letters you printed.
Then sprinkle with glitter or sand.

Name _____

A is for Alligator

Trace each **A** and **a** that you can find in the picture.
Color both sides of the alligator. Cut out the alligator.
Fold it in half. Bend the feet so the alligator stands up.

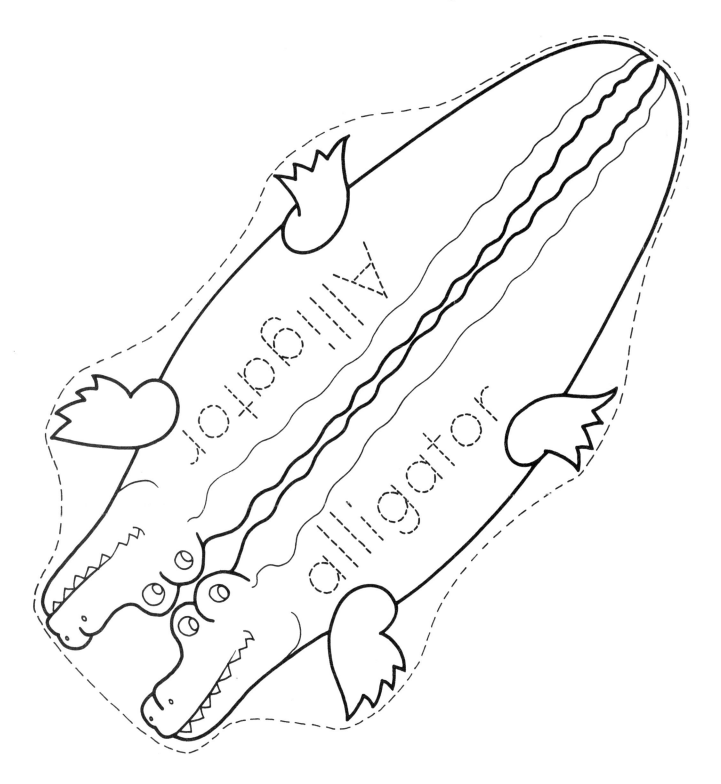

Name _____

Learning Bb

Color the letters below.

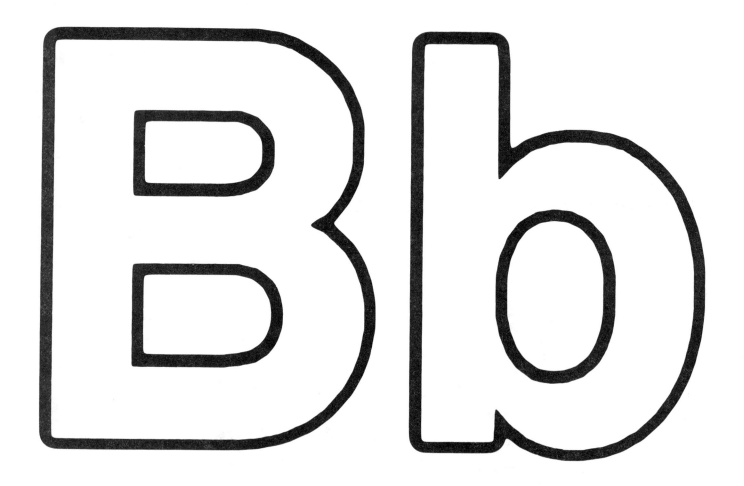

Writing Bb

Name _____

Look at the sentence below.
Trace each **B** and **b** that you can find.

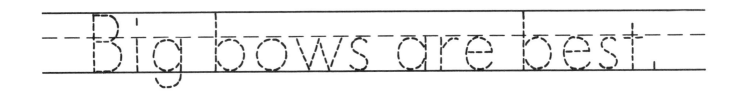

Color the bow.
Print **B** and **b** beside the bow.
Put glue on the letters you printed.
Then sprinkle with glitter or sand.

B is for Beach Ball

Name _____

Trace each **B** and **b** that you can find below the picture.
Make tissue balls by rolling pieces of tissue paper between your hands. Put glue on the beach ball.
Glue the tissue balls on the beach ball. Make the stripes different colors.

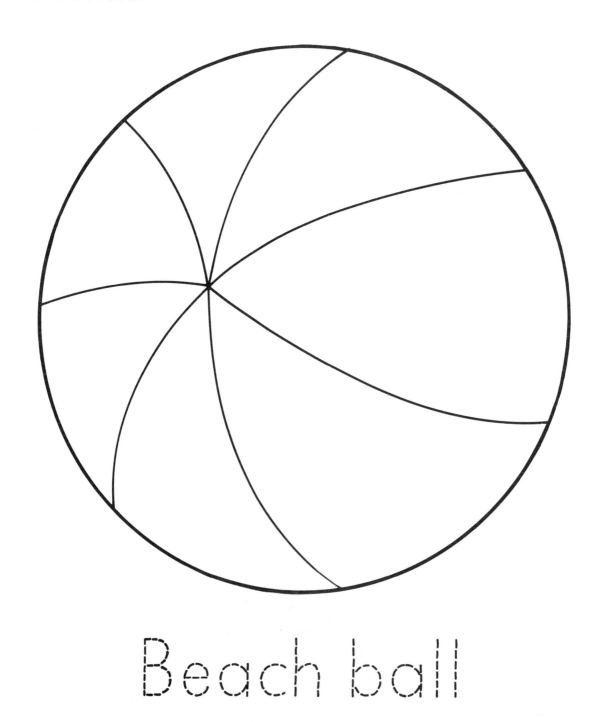

Beach ball

Name _____

Color the letters below.

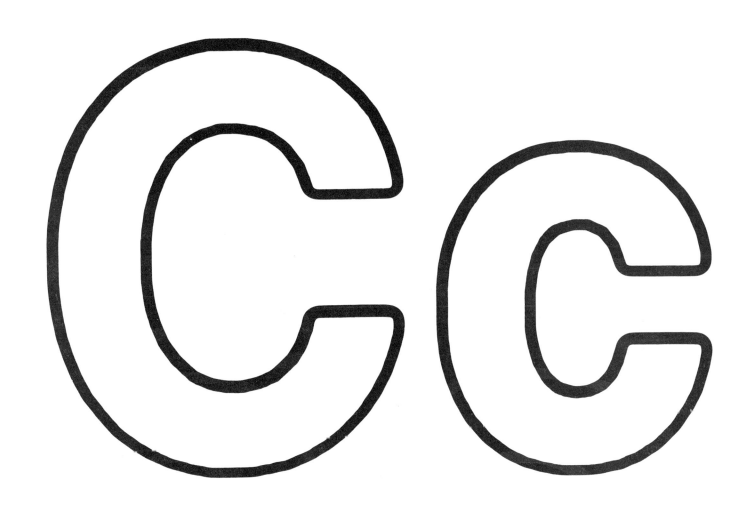

Writing Cc

Name _____

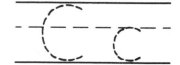

Look at the sentence below.
Trace each **C** and **c** that you can find.

Color the car.
Print **C** and **c** beside the car.
Put glue on the letters you printed.
Then sprinkle with glitter or sand.

C is for Cow

Name _____

Trace each **C** and **c** that you can find in the picture. Color the head and body of the cow.
On the dotted lines, cut out the head and body.
Glue the head on the bottom of a paper bag.
Glue the body below the head.
Put your hand inside the bag.
Make your cow puppet talk!

Letters A–Z © 1988

19

C is for Cow *(continued)*

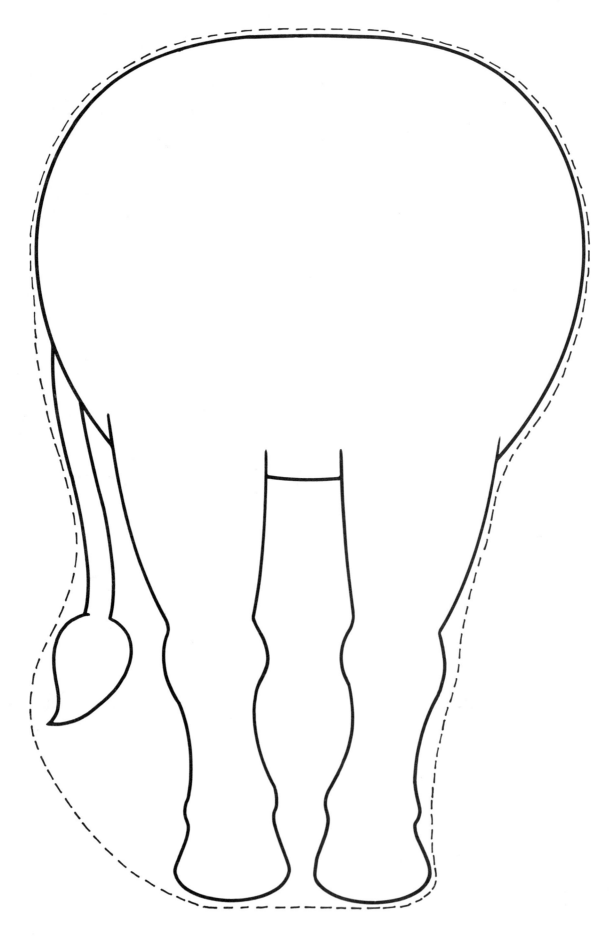

Name _____

Learning Dd

Color the letters below.

Writing Dd

Name _____

Look at the sentence below.
Trace each **D** and **d** that you can find.

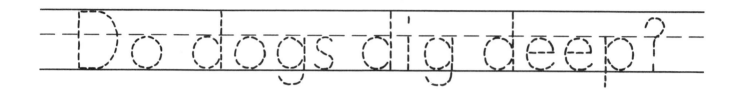

Color the dog.
Print **D** and **d** beside the dog.
Put glue on the letters you printed.
Then sprinkle with glitter or sand.

22

Letters A-Z © 1988

Name _____

D is for Doll

Trace each **D** and **d** that you can find in the picture.
Color the front and back of the doll.
Cut out both pieces.

Letters A-Z © 1988

23

D is for Doll *(continued)*

Staple the body together. Leave the head open.
Stuff the doll with cotton.
Staple the head closed.

Name _____

Learning Ee

Color the letters below.

Letters A–Z © 1988

Writing Ee

Name _____

Look at the sentence below.
Trace each **E** and **e** that you can find.

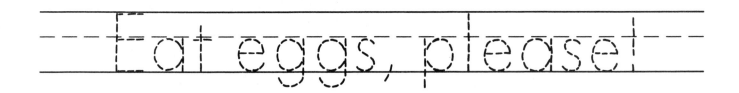

Color the egg.
Print **E** and **e** beside the egg.
Put glue on the letters you printed.
Then sprinkle with glitter or sand.

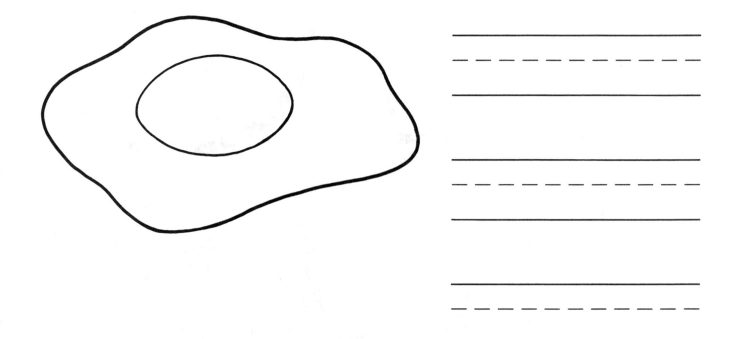

E is for Elephant

Name _____

Trace each **E** and **e** that you can find in the picture.
Color both sides of the elephant.
Cut out the elephant. Fold it in half.

Letters A–Z © 1988

27

Name _____

Learning Ff

Color the letters below.

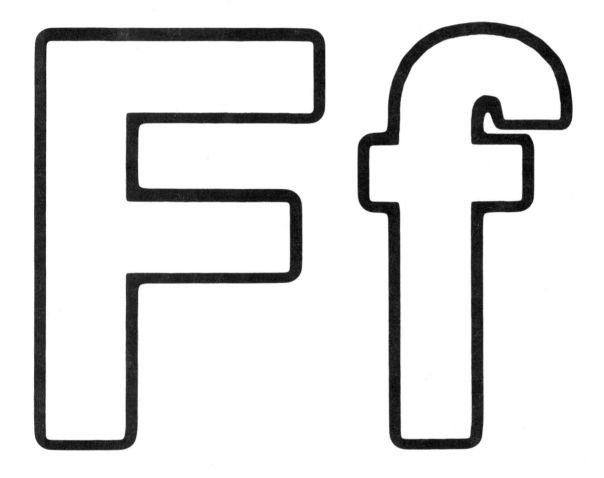

Writing Ff

Name _____

Look at the sentence below.
Trace each **F** and **f** that you can find.

Color the fire.
Print **F** and **f** beside the fire.
Put glue on the letters you print.
Then sprinkle with glitter or sand.

Letters A-Z © 1988                                              29

F is for Flower

Name _____

Trace each **F** and **f** that you can find below.
Color the flower parts.
Cut out the flower petals
and the circle.
Fold each petal.
Paste the ends together.
Paste the petals around
the circle above the stem.
Paste the cutout circle on
top of the other circle.

F is for Flower *(continued)*

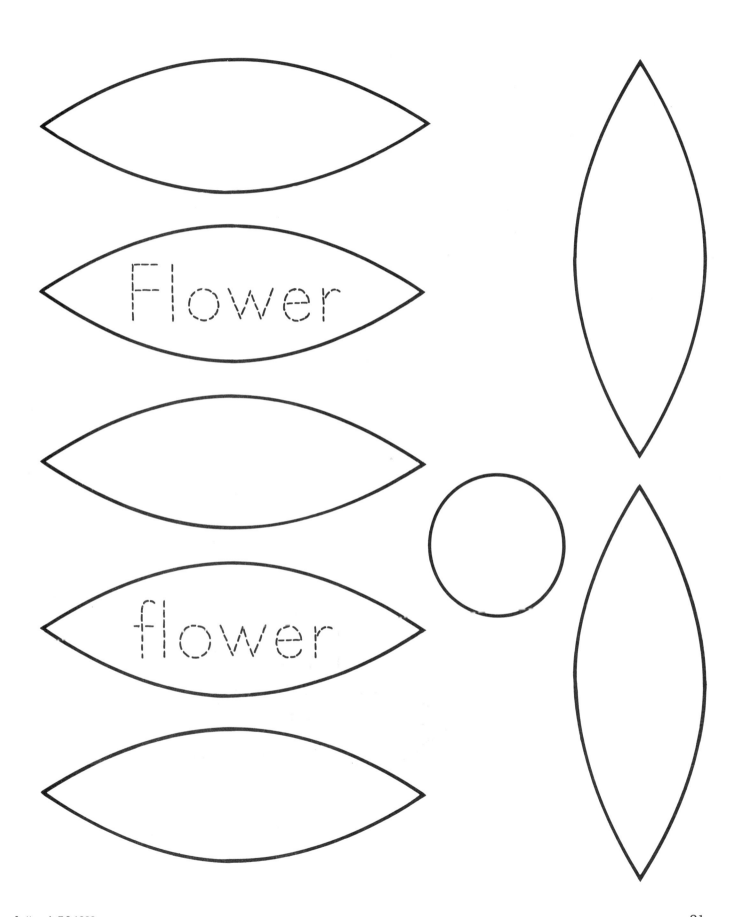

Name _____

Learning Gg

Color the letters below.

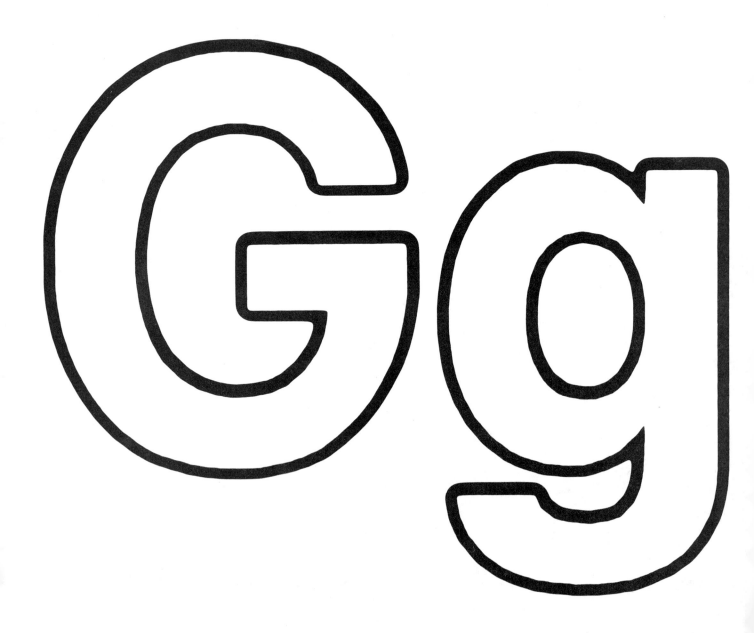

Writing Gg

Name _____

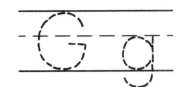

Look at the sentence below.
Trace each **G** and **g** that you can find.

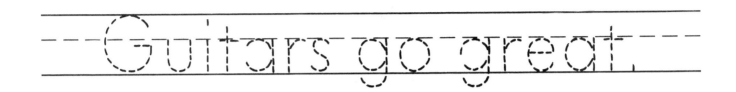

Color the guitar.
Print **G** and **g** beside the guitar.
Put glue on the letters you printed.
Then sprinkle with glitter or sand.

G is for Goldfish

Name _____

Trace each **G** and **g** that you can find below the picture.
Color the fins of the goldfish.
Glue orange tissue paper on the body of the goldfish.

Goldy goldfish

34

Letters A-Z © 1988

Name _____

Learning Hh

Color the letters below.

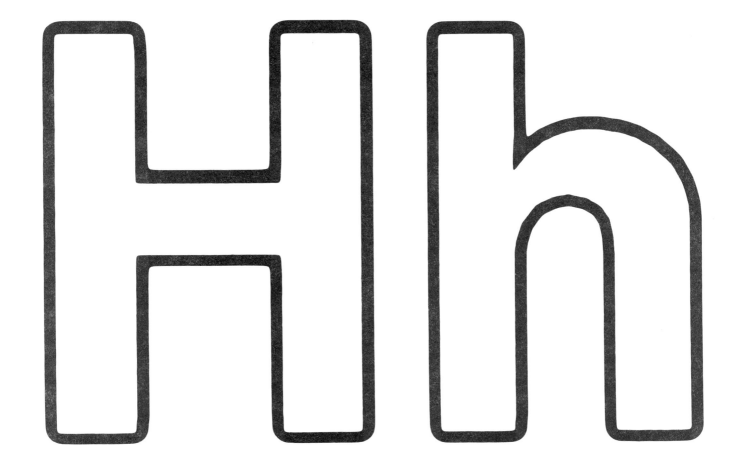

Name _____

Writing Hh

Look at the sentence below.
Trace each **H** and **h** that you can find.

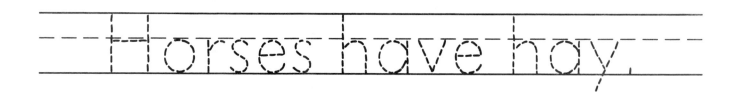

Color the horse.
Print **H** and **h** beside the horse.
Put glue on the letters you printed.
Then sprinkle with glitter or sand.

Name _____

H is for House

Color the parts of the house.
Trace each **H** and **h** that you can find.
Cut out the parts.
Glue them on another piece of paper
to make a house with trees.

Happy
house

Letters A–Z © 1988

Learning Ii

Name _____

Color the letters below.

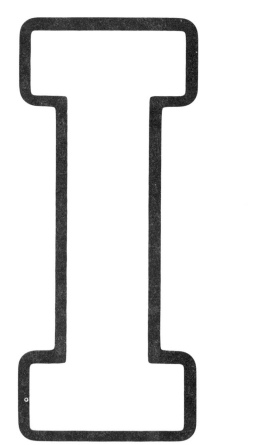 

Writing Ii

Name _____

Look at the sentence below.
Trace each **I** and **i** that you can find.

Color the insect.
Print **I** and **i** beside the insect.
Put glue on the letters you printed.
Then sprinkle with glitter or sand.

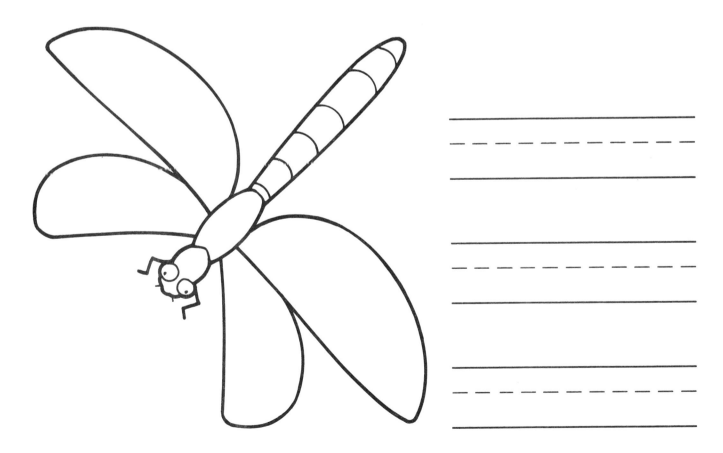

I is for Inchworm

Name _____

Trace each **I** and **i** that you can find below in the picture.
Color the tree branch and the circles. Cut out the circles.
Glue the circles on top of the black squares.
Draw a face on the inchworm.

Incredible inchworm

40

I is for Inchworm *(continued)*

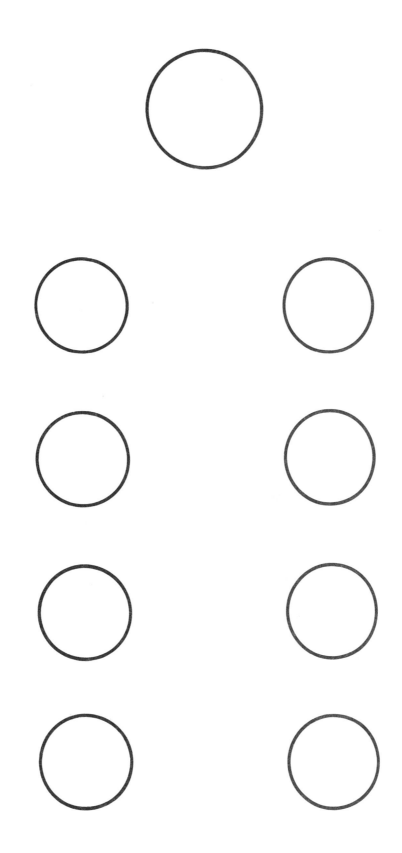

41

Name _____

Learning Jj

Color the letters below.

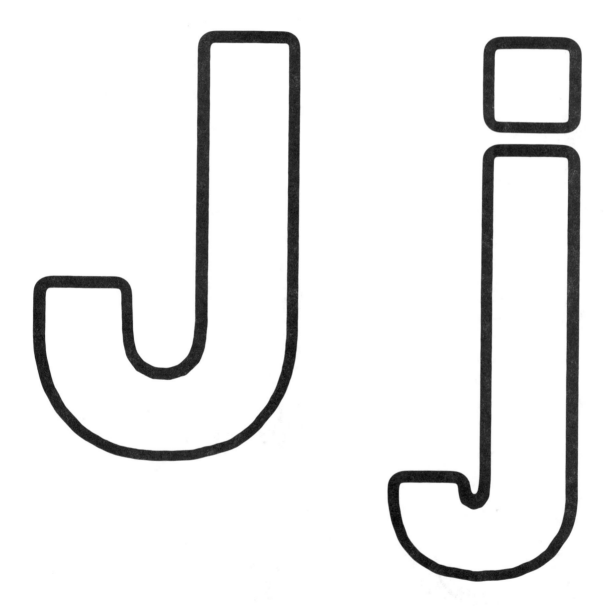

Writing Jj

Name _____

Look at the sentence below.
Trace each **J** and **j** that you can find.

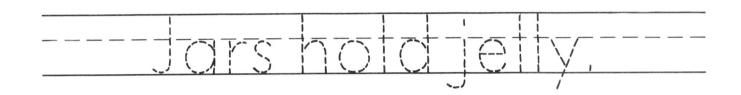

Color the jar.
Print **J** and **j** beside the jar.
Put glue on the letters you printed.
Then sprinkle with glitter or sand.

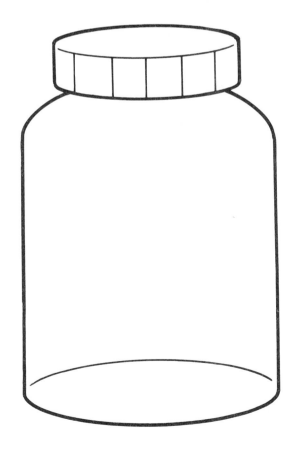

Letters A–Z © 1988

43

J is for Jellyfish

Name _____

Trace each **J** and **j** that you can find below the picture. Color the jellyfish. Glue the end of a piece of yarn on each black dot.

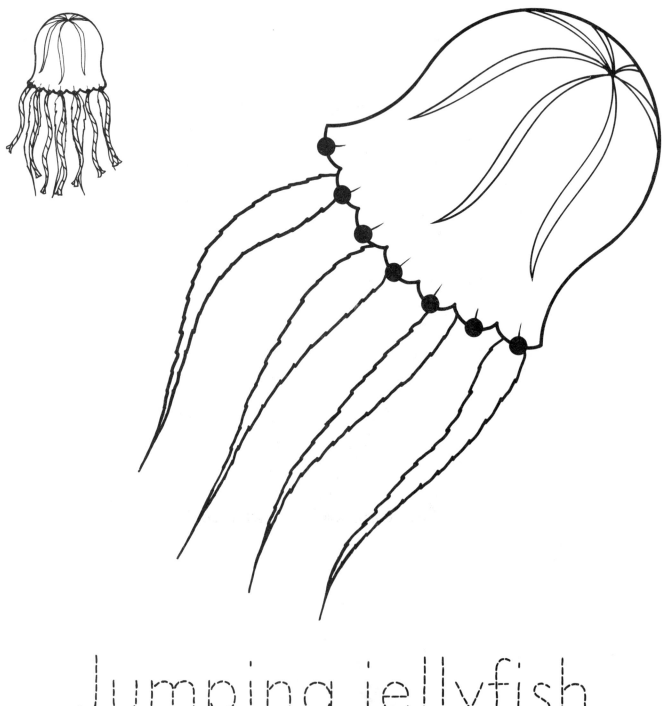

Jumping jellyfish

Learning Kk

Name _____

Color the letters below.

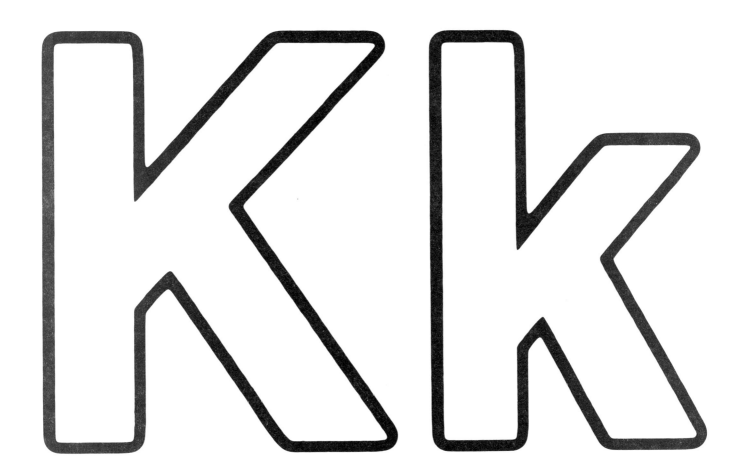

Letters A–Z © 1988

45

Writing Kk

Name _____

Look at the sentence below.
Trace each **K** and **k** that you can find.

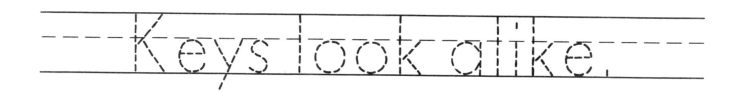

Color the key.
Print **K** and **k** beside the key.
Put glue on the letters you printed.
Then sprinkle with glitter or sand.

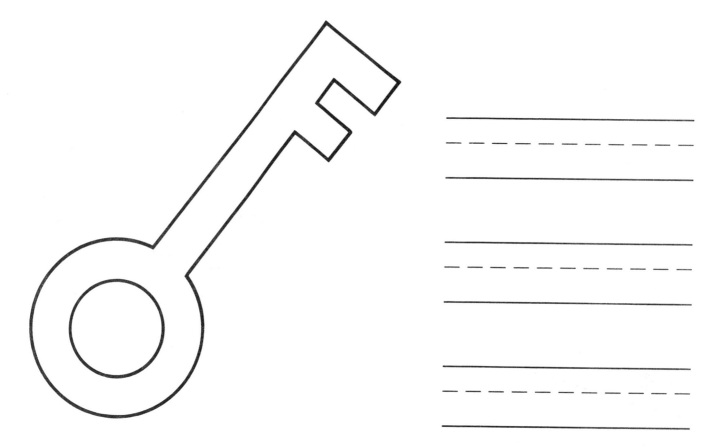

46

K is for Kite

Name _____

Trace each **K** and **k** that you can find in the picture.
Color the kite. Cut it out.
Glue the end of a piece of yarn on the dot.
Tie strips of cloth on the yarn.

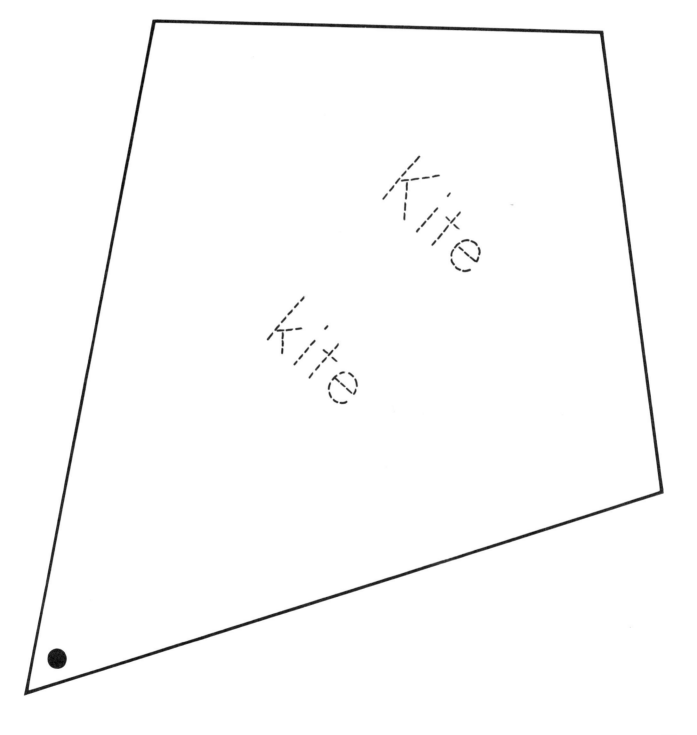

Name _____

Learning Ll

Color the letters below.

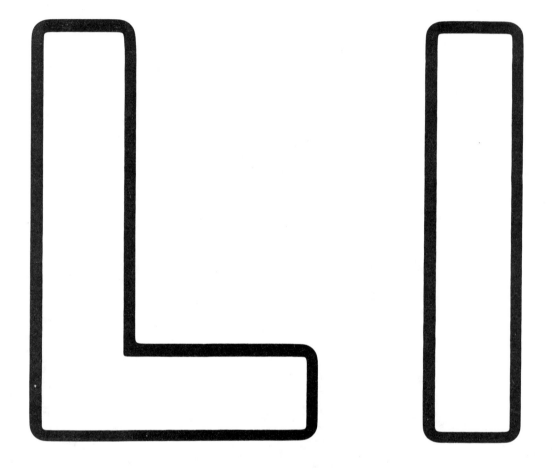

Writing Ll

Name _____

Look at the sentence below.
Trace each **L** and **I** that you can find.

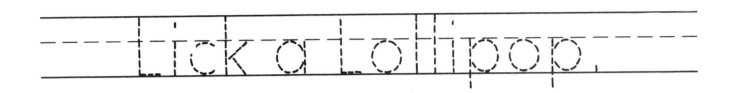

Color the lollipop.
Print **L** and **l** beside the lollipop.
Put glue on the letters you printed.
Then sprinkle with glitter or sand.

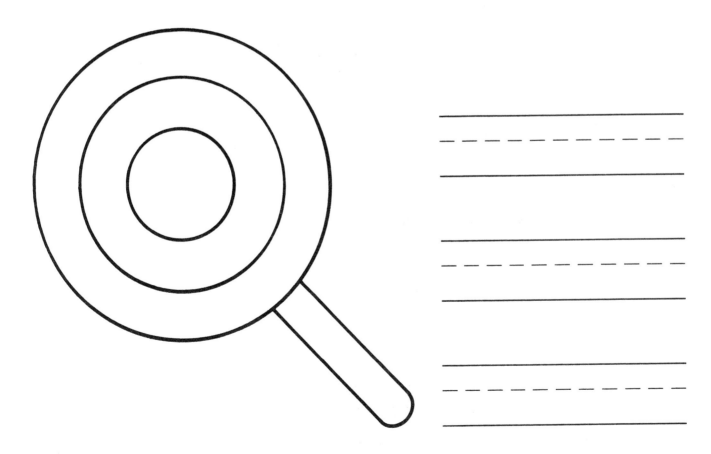

L is for Lobster

Name _____

Trace each **L** and **I** that you can find below the picture.
Color the lobster.
Put drops of glue on the lobster's body.
Sprinkle glitter over the lobster.

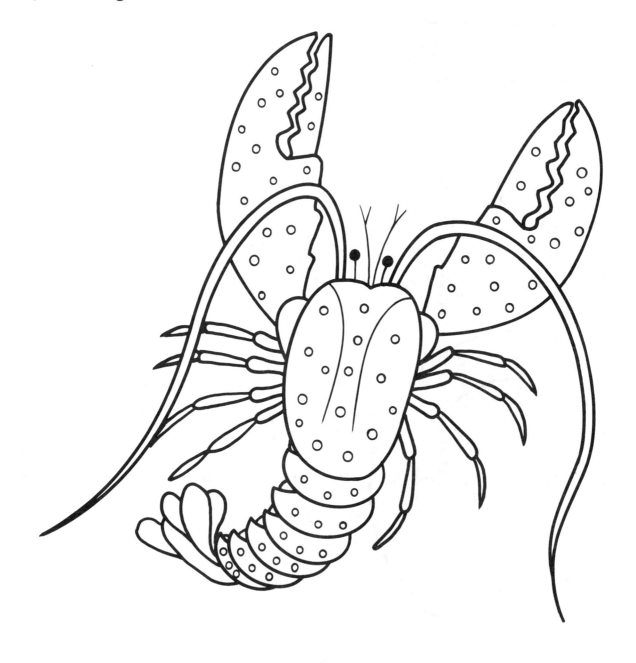

Lovely lobster

Learning Mm

Name _____

Color the letters below.

Writing Mm

Name _____

Mm

Look at the sentence below.
Trace each **M** and **m** that you can find.

Make a moonbeam.

Color the moon and star.
Print **M** and **m** beside the moon.
Put glue on the letters you printed.
Then sprinkle with glitter or sand.

M is for Mouse

Name _____

Trace each **M** and **m** that you can find in the picture.
Color the body and ears of the mouse. Cut them out.
Glue a piece of yarn inside the mouse shape.
Fold the body in half and glue it together.
Glue the ears on. Glue yarn on for whiskers and tail.

Learning Nn

Name _____

Color the letters below.

Writing Nn

Name _____

Look at the sentence below.
Trace each **N** and **n** that you can find.

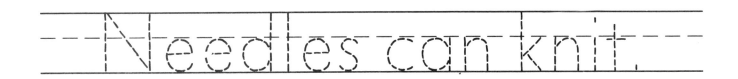

Color the needle.
Print **N** and **n** beside the needle.
Put glue on the letters you printed.
Then sprinkle with glitter or sand.

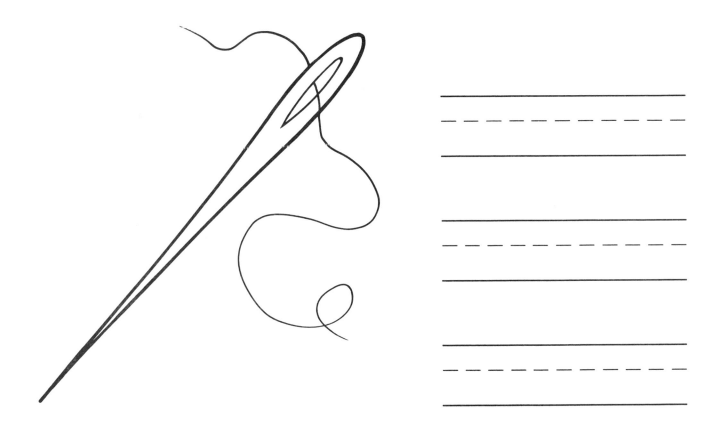

Letters A–Z © 1988

55

N is for Necklace

Name _____

Trace each **N** and **n** that you can find below the picture.
Make tissue balls by rolling pieces of tissue paper between your hands.
Put glue on the circles in the necklace.
Glue the tissue balls on. Make the necklace colorful.

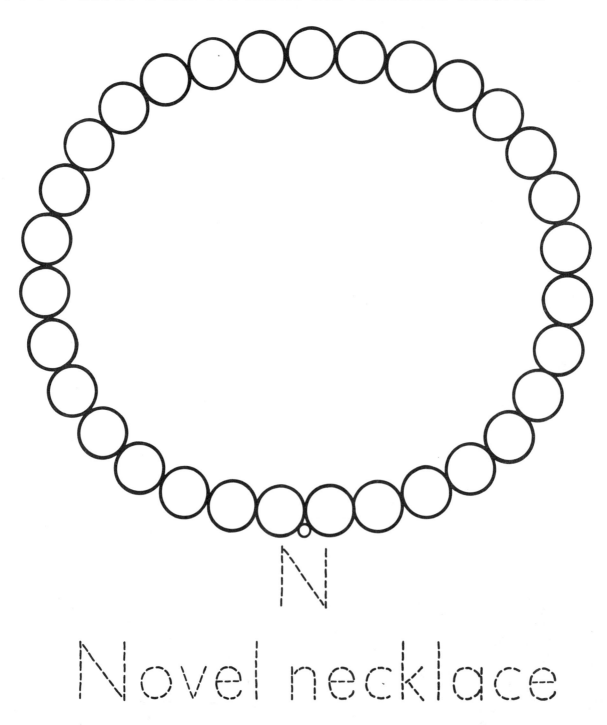

Novel necklace

Name _____

Learning Oo

Color the letters below.

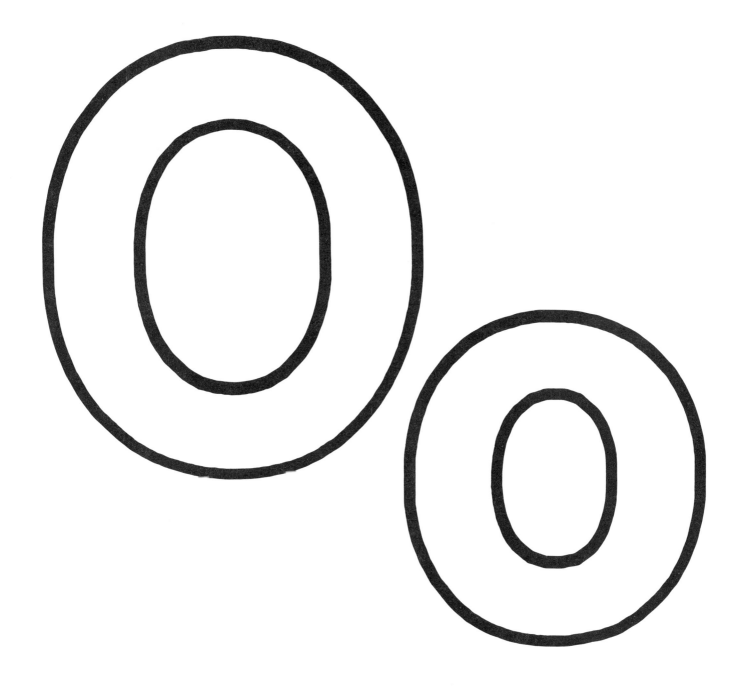

Writing Oo

Name _____

Look at the sentence below.
Trace each **O** and **o** that you can find.

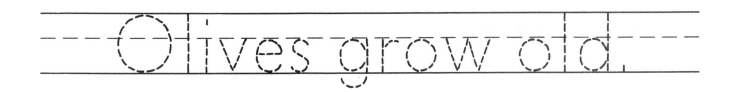

Color the olive.
Print **O** and **o** beside the olive.
Put glue on the letters you printed.
Then sprinkle with glitter or sand.

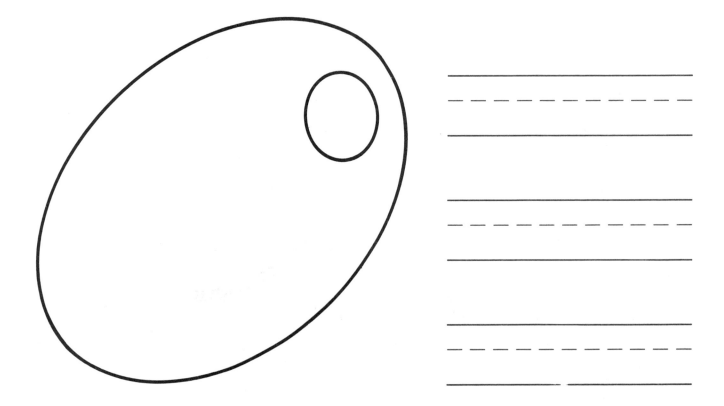

O is for Ostrich

Name _____

Trace each **O** and **o** that you can find in the picture.
Color the ostrich parts and cut them out.
Glue the big oval in the middle of a big piece of paper.
Glue yarn for the legs and attach the feet.
Glue yarn for the neck.
Glue the head and beak on.
Draw a face on the ostrich.
Glue feathers or more yarn for the tail.

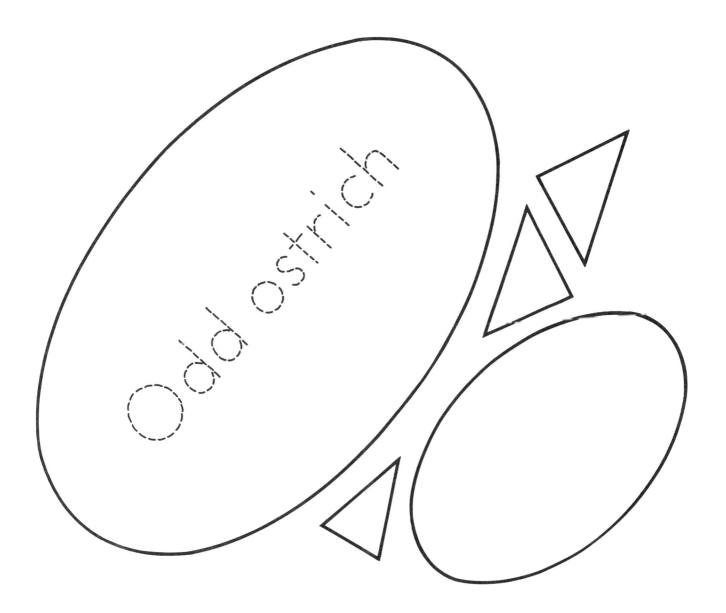

Learning Pp

Name _____

Color the letters below.

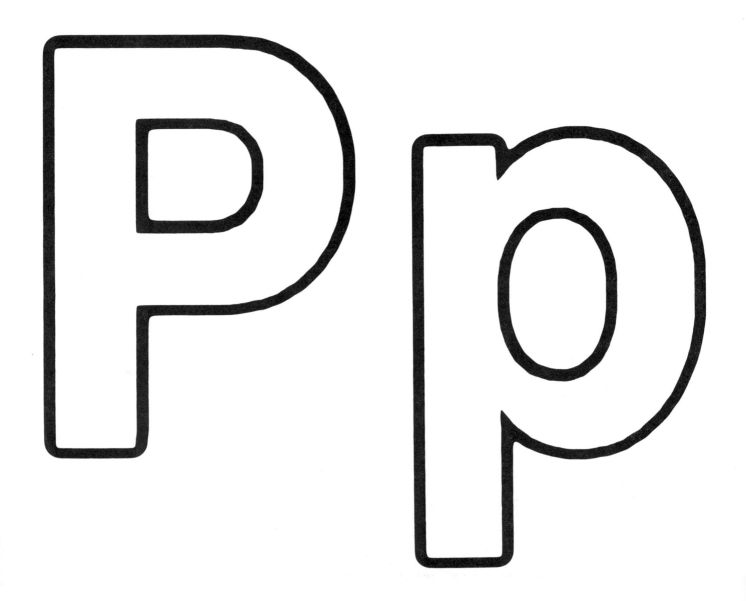

Writing Pp

Name _____

Look at the sentence below.
Trace each **P** and **p** that you can find.

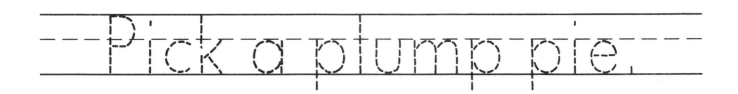

Color the pie.
Print **P** and **p** beside the pie.
Put glue on the letters you printed.
Then sprinkle with glitter or sand.

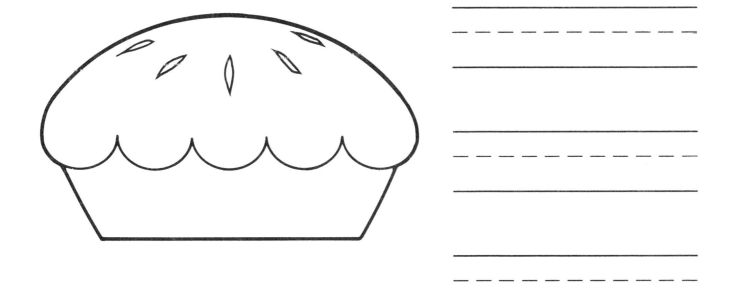

P is for Pig

Name _____

Trace each **P** and **p** that you can find in the picture.
Color the shapes and cut them out.
Glue the big circle on a piece of paper.
Make a curly tail by cutting on the
dotted line inside the small circle.
Glue the tail at the top of the big circle.
Glue on the other parts for the head,
nose, and ears.
Draw a face and legs on the pig.

Learning Qq

Name _____

Color the letters below.

Writing Qq

Name _____

Look at the sentence below.
Trace each **Q** and **q** that you can find.

Quarters go quickly.

Color the quarter.
Print **Q** and **q** beside the quarter.
Put glue on the letters you printed.
Then sprinkle with glitter or sand.

Q is for Queen

Name _____

Trace each **Q** and **q** that you can find below.
Color the queen.
Glue sequins and glitter on her dress and crown.

Queen Jacqueline

Name _____

Color the letters below.

Writing Rr

Name _____

Look at the sentence below.
Trace each **R** and **r** that you can find.

Color the rainbow.
Print **R** and **r** beside the rainbow.
Put glue on the letters you printed.
Then sprinkle with glitter or sand.

R is for Rabbit

Name _____

Trace each **R** and **r** that you can find in the picture.
Color the head and body of the rabbit. Cut them out. Glue the head on the bottom of a paper bag.
Glue the body below the head.
Glue yarn for the rabbit's whiskers.
Glue a cotton ball on the back of the bag for a tail.
Put your hand inside the bag.
Make your rabbit puppet talk.

R is for Rabbit (continued)

Letters A–Z © 1988

Name _____

Learning Ss

Color the letters below.

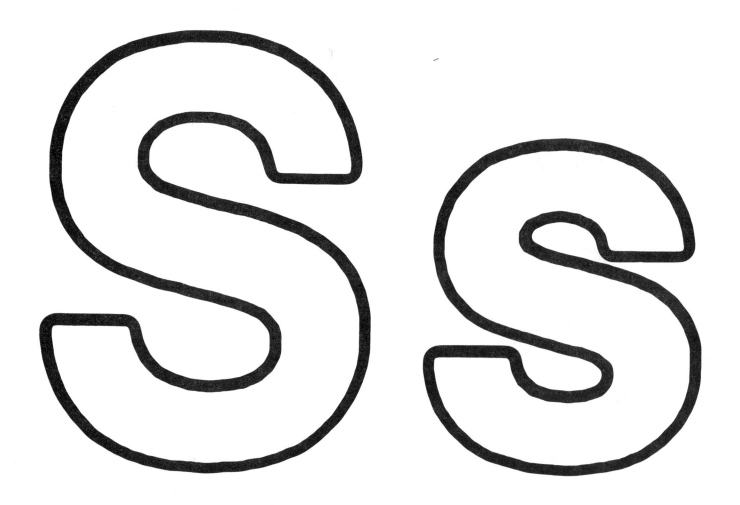

Writing Ss

Name _____

Look at the sentence below.
Trace each **S** and **s** that you can find.

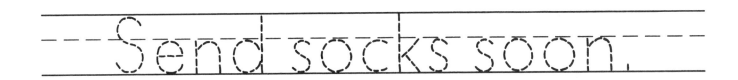

Color the sock.
Print **S** and **s** beside the sock.
Put glue on the letters you printed.
Then sprinkle with glitter or sand.

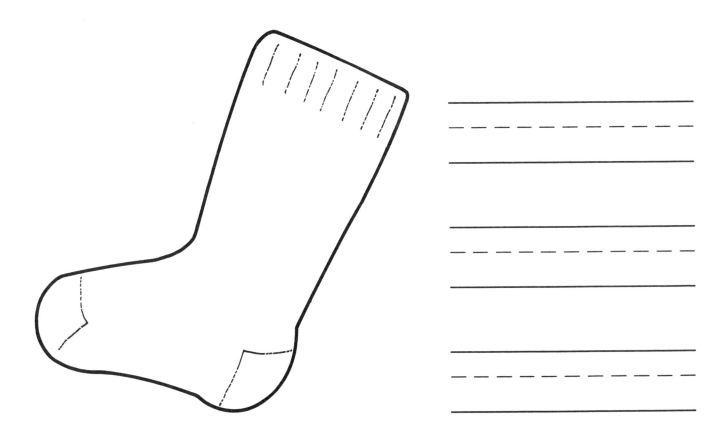

Letters A–Z © 1988   71

S is for Snake

Name _____

Trace each **S** and **s** that you can find in the picture.
Color both sides of the snake.
Cut out the snake along the broken line.
Fold it in half so the snake stands up.

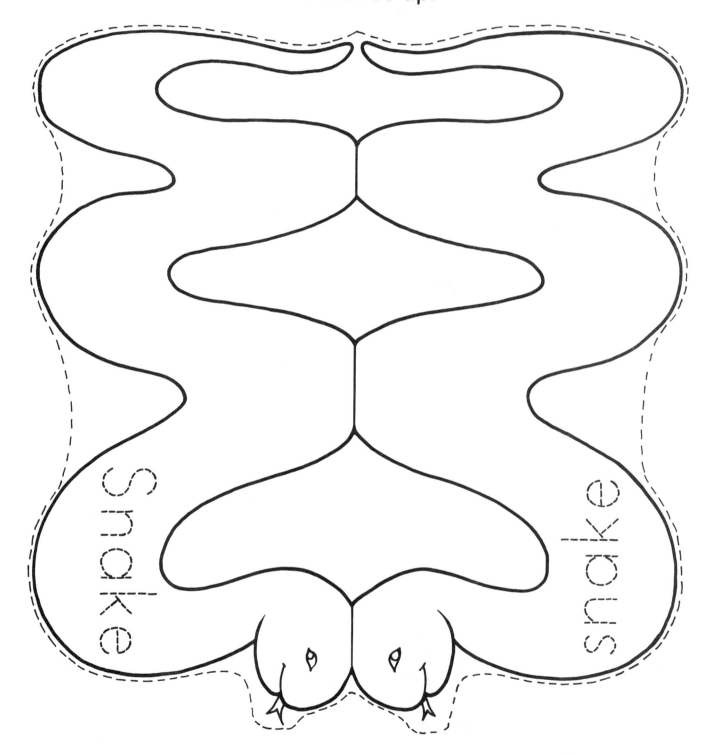

72

Letters A–Z © 1988

Name _____

Learning Tt

Color the letters below.

Writing Tt

Name _____

Look at the sentence below.
Trace each **T** and **t** that you can find.

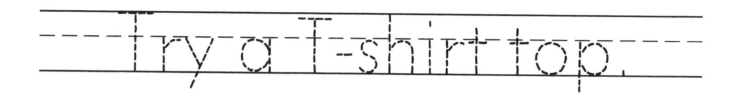

Color the T-shirt.
Print **T** and **t** beside the T-shirt.
Put glue on the letters you printed.
Then sprinkle with glitter or sand.

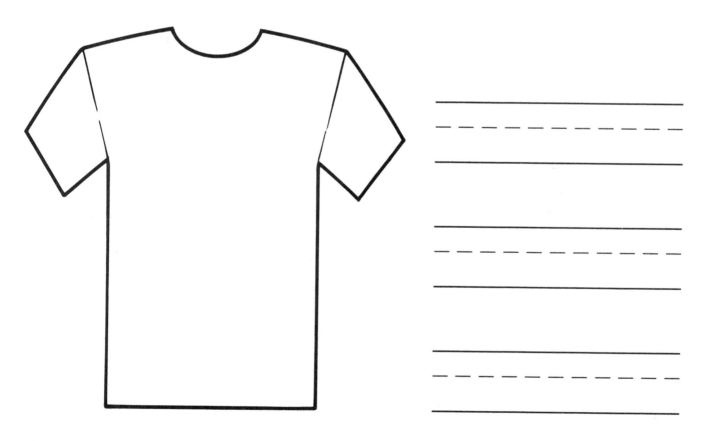

T is for Turtle

Name _____

Trace each **T** and **t** that you can find below the picture.
Color both sides of the turtle. Cut out the turtle.
Fold it in half. Bend the feet so the turtle stands up.

Name _____

Learning Uu

Color the letters below.

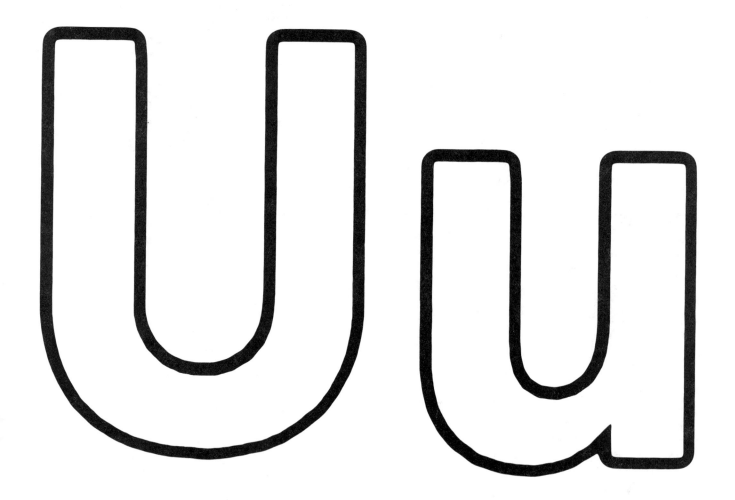

Writing Uu

Name _____

Look at the sentence below.
Trace each **U** and **u** that you can find.

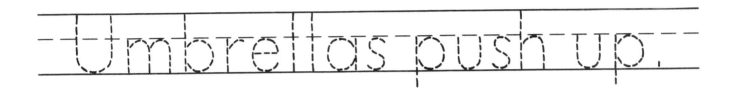

Color the umbrella.
Print **U** and **u** beside the umbrella.
Put glue on the letters you printed.
Then sprinkle with glitter or sand.

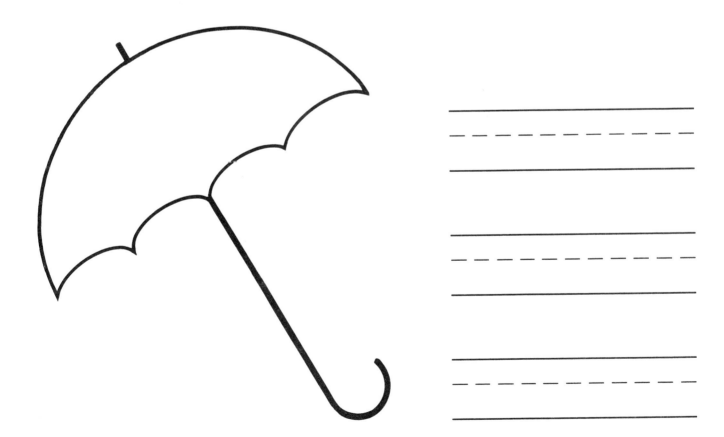

U is for Underwater

Name _____

Trace each **U** and **u** that you can find below the picture.
Color the picture in heavy crayon.
Paint over the picture with watercolors.
Then let the picture dry.

Uncle Octopus

78

Letters A–Z © 1988

Name _____

Color the letters below.

Writing Vv

Name _____

Look at the sentence below.
Trace each **V** and **v** that you can find.

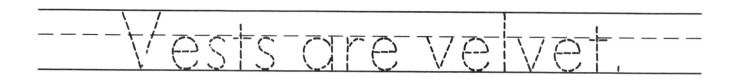

Color the vest.
Print **V** and **v** beside the vest.
Put glue on the letters you printed.
Then sprinkle with glitter or sand.

V is for Volcano

Name _____

Trace each **V** and **v** that you can find below the picture.
Color the volcano. Curl pieces of tissue paper.
Glue them to the volcano smoke.
Put glue on the sides of the volcano.
Then sprinkle with sand.

Letters A–Z © 1988

81

Name _____

Learning Ww

Color the letters below.

Writing Ww

Name _____

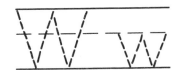

Look at the sentence below.
Trace each **W** and **w** that you can find.

Watermelons grow.

Color the watermelon.
Print **W** and **w** beside the watermelon.
Put glue on the letters you printed.
Then sprinkle with glitter or sand.

Name _____

W is for Witch

Trace each **W** and **w** that you can find on the parts of the witch.
Color the parts. Cut them out.
Glue the parts on a large piece of paper, matching up the black dots.
Glue the hands, feet, and head on the witch.
Glue yarn for hair, and glue on the hat.
Draw a face.

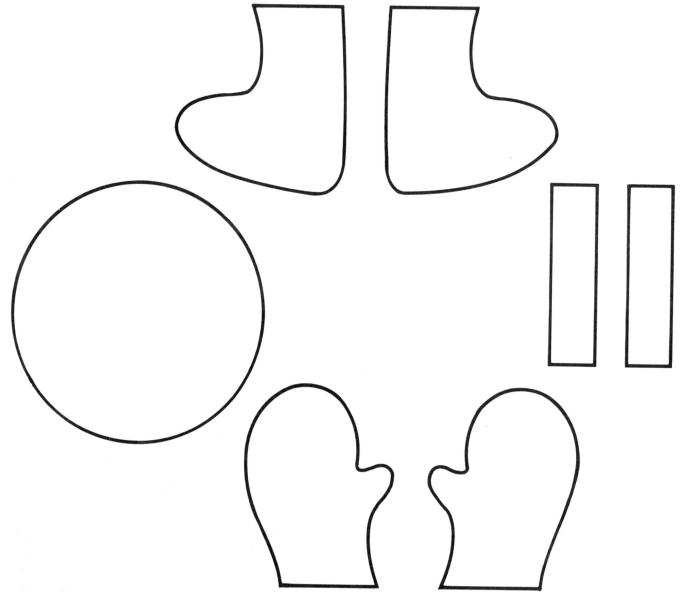

84

Letters A–Z © 1988

W is for Witch *(continued)*

Letters A–Z © 1988

85

Name _____

Learning Xx

Color the letters below.

Writing Xx

Name _____

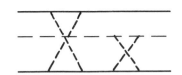

Look at the sentence below.
Trace each **X** and **x** that you can find.

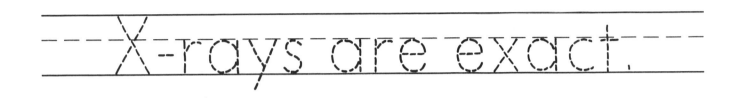

Color the x-ray of this extinct reptile.
Print **X** and **x** beside the x-ray.
Put glue on the letters you printed.
Then sprinkle with glitter or sand.

X is for Xylophone

Name _____

Trace each **X** and **x** that you can find below the picture.
Color the xylophone and the xylophone keys.
Cut out the xylophone keys.
Glue the keys in the correct places on the xylophone.

Exotic Xylophone

X is for Xylophone *(continued)*

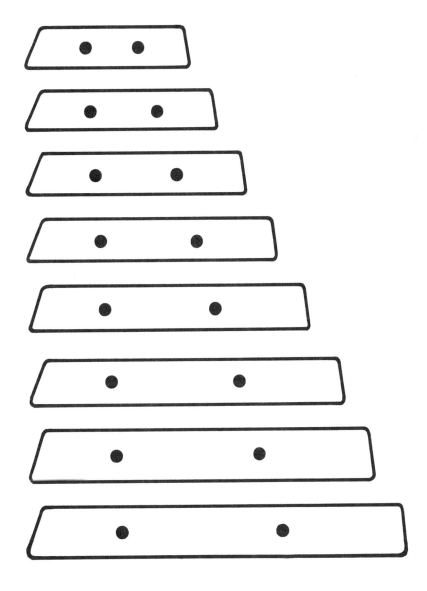

*Letters A–Z* © 1988

89

Name _____

Learning Yy

Color the letters below.

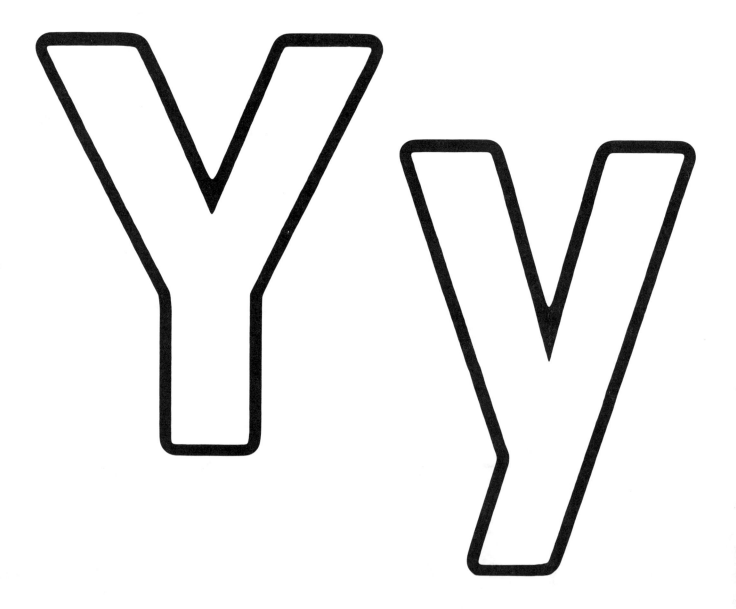

Writing Yy

Name _____

Look at the sentence below.
Trace each **Y** and **y** that you can find.

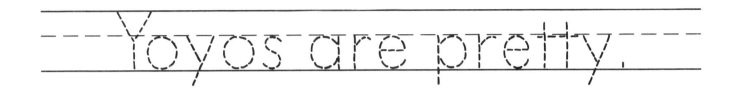

Color the yoyo.
Print **Y** and **y** beside the yoyo.
Put glue on the letters you printed.
Then sprinkle with glitter or sand.

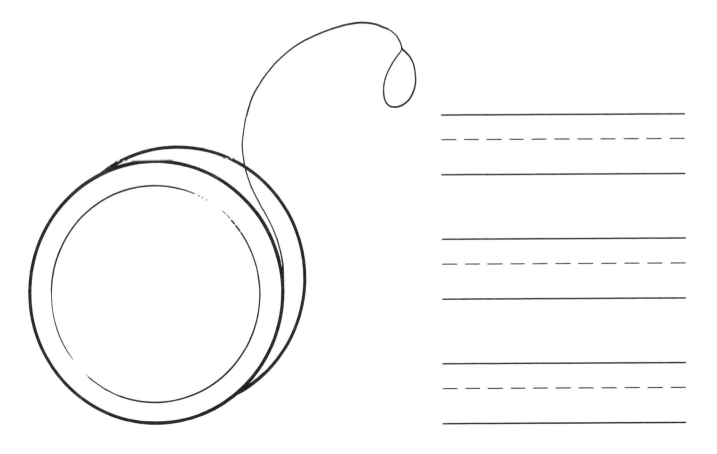

Y is for Yak

Name _____

Trace each **Y** and **y** that you can find below the picture.
Color the yak yellow.
Glue yellow yarn on the yak.

Yellow yarn yak

Name _____

Learning Zz

Color the letters below.

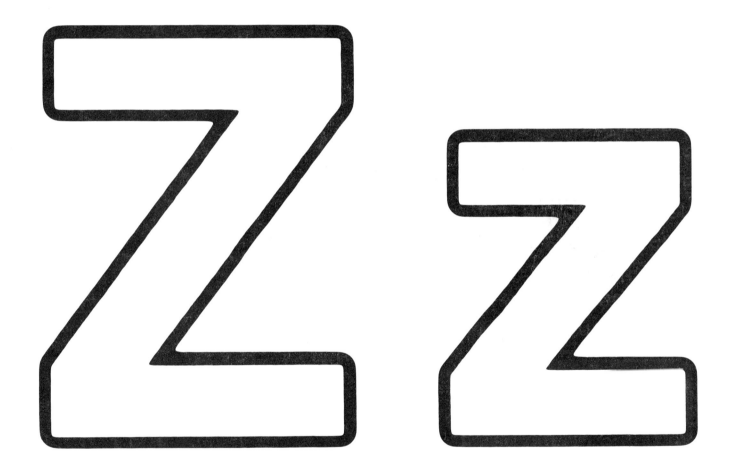

Writing Zz

Name _____

Look at the sentence below.
Trace each **Z** and **z** that you can find.

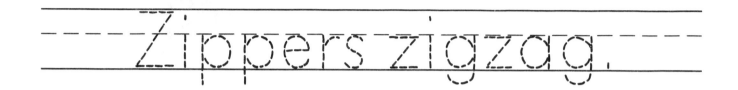

Color the zipper.
Print **Z** and **z** beside the zipper.
Put glue on the letters you printed.
Then sprinkle with glitter or sand.

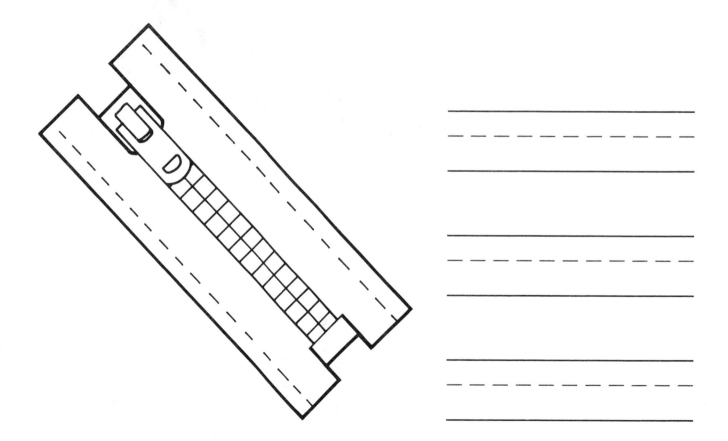

Z is for Zebra

Name _____

Trace each **Z** and **z** that you can find in the picture.
Color the head and body of the zebra.
Then cut them out.
Glue the head on the bottom of a paper bag.
Glue the body below the head.
Put your hand inside the bag.
Make your zebra puppet talk.

Zany
zebra

Z is for Zebra *(continued)*

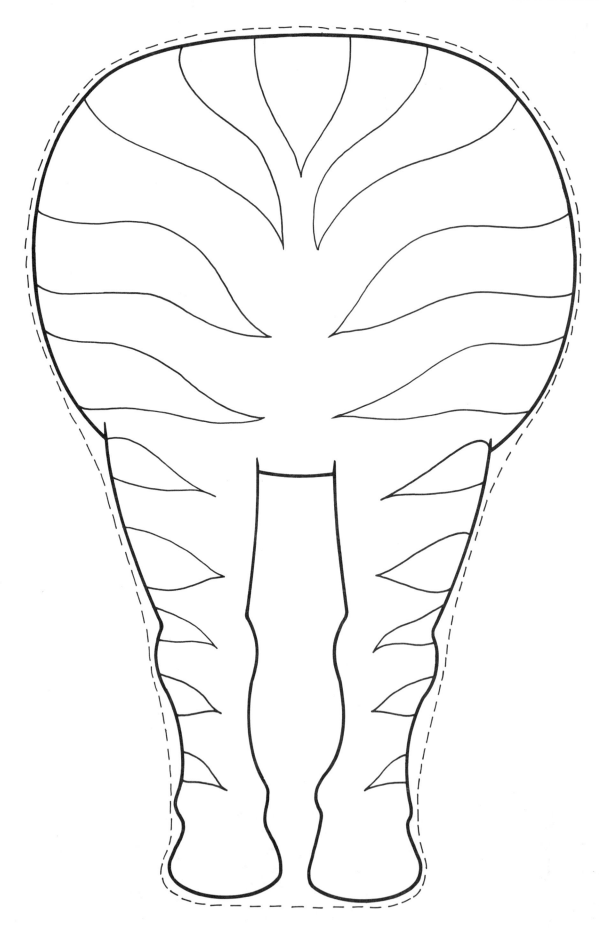

96

Letters A–Z © 1988